To To

w...

This is ...nd me down
book; you hand it down to
anyone in the family with
a 2 year old.

love mum!
x x x

To Ali & Aimi,

time to pass down
the bible of mum?

I'm so happy you are
all ok, I'm here always
no matter... you are
a "fam" so cool...

→ all "WILL" be ok
Ali   first stresspull + what
you got, but all will
be OK.... love you ♡

pass this on to the next?

50 WAYS TO TAME A TODDLER

hamlyn

50 WAYS TO TAME A TODDLER

HOW TO CHARM AND DISARM YOUR DIMINUTIVE ADVERSARY

An Hachette UK Company
www.hachette.co.uk

First published in Great Britain in 2009 by
Hamlyn, a division of Octopus Publishing Group Ltd
2–4 Heron Quays, London E14 4JP
www.octopusbooks.co.uk

ISBN 978-0-600-61990-1

A CIP catalogue record for this book is available from
the British Library

Printed and bound in China

10 9 8 7 6 5 4 3 2 1

CONTENTS

INTRODUCTION

We've all heard about the 'Terrible Twos'. What people don't tell you is that the fun and games often begin somewhat earlier and may continue into the 'Troublesome Threes' and the 'Feisty Fours'. And of course everyone knows adults whose behaviour suggests they have never quite outgrown the infantile phase.

If you are struggling to tame a tireless toddler and her erratic behaviour is wearing you down, take solace in the fact that you are not alone and that little miscreants across the globe are flexing their muscles and squaring up to their parents for another bout in the battle of wills.

In this book you will find a host of tried-and-tested strategies for dealing with 50 situations in which tiny terrors are likely to disturb the peace. Forewarned is forearmed – good luck!

THE NATURE OF THE BEAST

Toddlers are as changeable as the wind and capable of unimaginable mischief. Beguiling angels one minute, they can transform within seconds into demented banshees, then be suspiciously quiet five minutes later. This means you constantly need to have your wits about you and understand who or what you are dealing with. More often than not, distraction is your best strategy, as you can capitalize on your child's short attention span and divert his energies.

Though you may suspect your toddler of hatching plans for world domination – your world, at least – she is not actually that forward thinking. The average toddler lives in the here and now, and is egocentric, firmly planted at the centre of her own universe. In other words, she is incapable of putting herself in

other people's shoes or anticipating their feelings or reactions. Toddlers are not simply little adults who know less – they process information quite differently from adults. Since they do not fully understand cause and effect, the way they choose to go about something is often only a best guess and the connections they make between events can be quite bizarre. Toddlers need to be taught the ways of the world and to have plenty of first-hand experiences before they can consistently behave in a civilized and logical manner.

POSITIVE PARENTING

According to the experts, positive parenting is all about making your role rewarding, effective and fun. This includes having the confidence to set boundaries for your child and stick to them. But when your child's favourite word is 'No', you may find it difficult to undestand exactly where the positive fits into parenting.

It's worth remembering that very small children do not mean to be naughty – they simply haven't learned to be good yet. The best way of making sure little ones learn to understand and abide by the rules is to praise them when they get it right and ignore, rather than punish, bad behaviour. This can involve you taking a pretty big leap of faith and probably several very deep breaths, but at the end of a long day you can reward yourself with a big gold star (or something a bit stronger, if you like) for your fortitude, patience and perseverance.

To brush up your parenting skills and keep yourself on track in times of duress, try keeping a handy list of winning strategies (see opposite) posted on your fridge door as a visual reminder.

WINNING STRATEGIES

- Use avoidance tactics – if possible, deflect a conflict situation through distraction.

- Find a routine – your child is more likely to behave if he has rules to follow and knows what to expect.

- Give rewards – pay him positive attention and praise him when he behaves well. Older children like getting stickers and star charts.

- Ask him nicely to do something – if he ignores you, ask him again firmly.

- Ignore him when he acts up so he doesn't use misbehaviour to seek attention.

- Stay calm – show him by example how to react to tricky situations.

- Issue warnings – explain the consequences to three- and four-year-olds and give them a chance to reconsider their course of action.

- Use time-out – as a last resort, removing an older child from a situation to reflect and calm down for a few minutes can work when all else has failed.

- Teach him to apologize – saying sorry and making up with a cuddle is the best way to move on.

A CAN-DO CHILD

Toddler taming is all about creating a happy, confident, can-do child (that doesn't mean one who can do exactly as he pleases). You may think your child currently needs no help whatsoever on the assertiveness front, but confidence is a fragile thing. Toddlerdom is fraught with frustration – not only are the basic skills lacking, but also the words come out all wrong and grown-ups just seem hell-bent on causing as much inconvenience as possible with their unreasonable demands and expectations. A public display of unbridled rage does not seem that out of order in the circumstances.

Children who know that they are loved for who they are, rather than for what they can do, develop self-esteem that allows them to take the rough with the smooth and try again when they fail at something. Above all they need to see your love through words and actions, and be supported and praised in order to learn and rise to the next challenge.

You are your son's or daughter's first and most important role model and that can seem like quite an onerous and intimidating responsibility! Although no one is perfect all of the time, being aware of setting a good example is a step in the right direction. And, by employing positive parenting strategies, you will be well on the way to success. Remember, too, that a little guile and flexibility never go amiss and you shouldn't feel too guilty if you occasionally bend the rules slightly or fail to live up to the standards you have set yourself. Now read on to find out how to take 50 situations in hand and be a can-do parent.

HAVOC &
HELL-RAISING

THE VOLUME BUTTON

A toddler's quiet button is not always fully operational, although it magically seems to function well when he's up to mischief. At full throttle his scream may reach 100 decibels plus, but more often than not you'll just hear him chatting to himself as he goes about his business.

- Toddler talk is to be encouraged, but he needs to know that sometimes you need some peace and quiet and that you will listen later.

- If you occasionally have to silence an over-talkative two-year-old, provide suitable diversions such as a pen and paper.

- A (healthy) snack may offer some respite from a barrage of noise pollution. Make sure it's not anything of a size or consistency he might choke on (toddlers don't have many teeth to chew with), and always supervise a young child eating.

MESS

With a toddler in the house your aesthetic standards will inevitably drop. Forget about tasteful decor – all that bright plastic that little children love will find its way into every room and destroy any semblance of order and colour schemes.

- The word 'tidy' will not enter her vocabulary unless you play a game of speed-sorting toys into boxes.

- Try to limit the amount of detritus by not getting everything out at once. Put toys aside and rotate them every so often in order to retain her interest.

- She doesn't always need a huge selection – a construction toy or some dressing-up clothes can keep her occupied for hours.

- Store her things in child-friendly drawers and cupboards so that she can take a few out at a time without tipping the whole lot on the floor.

- Many toys are spoiled by broken or missing parts, so try to reunite all the bits each time you tidy up.

WRITING ON THE WALL

It is good to encourage your child's creative side but no parent wants their toddler's abstract expressionism daubed all over the living-room walls. Little children love to scribble and can't resist a blank canvas, so you will need to keep an eye on her 'decorating' projects.

- Ensure her pens and paints are non-toxic, water-based and washable.

- Recycle cartons and paper for her to use for her artistic creations.

- Buy her an artist's easel.

- Protect tables and floors with newspaper in case of Jackson Pollock-style drips and splatters.

- Make her aware that the majority of books are *not* intended for colouring in!

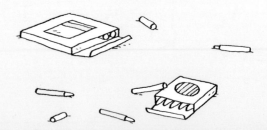

DEMOLITION

When he's not throwing things, your toddler is probably bashing them. This tends to be a boy thing – an evolutionary throwback to man's hunter-gatherer past, perhaps – and inevitably involves a lot of noise.

- Buy him a wooden mallet and pegboard so he can hammer away to his heart's content.

- Issue the rest of the family with hard hats and earplugs if he shows signs of threatening behaviour or if the din gets too loud.

- Make sure he realizes you prefer your things the way they are – not dismantled or destroyed.

- Keep precious objects out of his reach and check that windows, furniture and doors are fitted with safety glass.

THROWING THINGS

Throwing and catching is an activity small children never tire of. So, long after a ball game is over, they look for anything else they can chuck around, and with what exciting results!

- The first time disaster strikes he is really just experimenting. Since he can't foresee the consequences of his actions, don't be too cross.

- Show him what he has broken and explain that now you have to clear it up.

- If he persists in doing the same thing, tell him off firmly and remove the missile.

- Remove all fragile objects within his range and if his aim is particularly good, enrol him in a local sports team – he could be their star player.

TURNING
ON THE TAPS

Your toddler getting into the habit of washing his
hands is something to be applauded. But, like so many
things, there is also a downside. Expect water to squirt
up the walls on a regular basis, the basin to overflow
at least once a week and the bar of soap to end up on
the floor about 90 per cent of the time.

- Turn the thermostat down so hot water can't scald
  him and always run cold water in the bath first.

- Swap your bar of soap for a liquid variety in a
  plastic pump dispenser.

- Help him to reach everything he needs with the aid
  of a sturdy footstool.

- Remind him not to leave the taps running and if he
  keeps forgetting, put up a visual reminder that he
  understands and can't miss.

- Convert your taps to the self-closing push kind
  before you experience one flood too many.

TANTRUMS

Parents who claim their children never have temper
tantrums are obviously either lying or bribing them.
When trouble is brewing, resist the temptation to
throw a tantrum of your own, and act your age –
that's all your toddler is doing. Try these tips for
reducing the frequency and intensity of toddler rage.

• Very small children have tantrums because they
  can't manage their emotions. They are too young to
  listen to reason, so, instead, use distraction and, if
  necessary, remove them from the situation; you can
  also try ignoring them. Give comfort and positive
  reinforcement but don't capitulate to their demands!

- Extreme behaviour such as head-banging and breath-holding require action to keep your child safe. Hold her firmly facing outwards with the back of her head against your chest and tell her quietly to calm down. Once she has mellowed, you can give her some positive attention.

- A short 'time out' (one minute for each year of her life) can work for an older child, as can rewarding good behaviour with stickers or a star chart. Give yourself a medal for remaining calm, too.

DIVA

You could be forgiven for thinking your toddler is in line for an Academy Award. But, although she appears to ham up her performance in adversity for all she's worth, she does genuinely experience heightened emotions and needs you to understand her suffering.

- Scraped knees, bumps and bruises are common occurrences. Keep a basic first-aid kit to hand and learn emergency procedures just in case.

- Minor aches and pains can often be soothed away with a cuddle and gentle reassurance.

- Show sympathy but don't overreact to minor upsets and injuries. If you remain calm your child is less likely to panic.

- If she is obviously 'putting it on' to seek attention, give her a quick cuddle or make her laugh and it will all soon be forgotten.

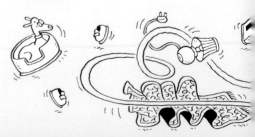

TURBO-CHARGED

You once fondly dreamt of the patter of tiny feet.
The reality is more like a bull in a china shop, as your
child rampages from room to room in a deranged
state of excitement. Toddlers are masters of making
a grand entrance.

- Fit slam stoppers around doors to prevent trapped
  fingers, and place stops behind doors to protect
  the walls.

- Cover sharp corners which he might run into.

- Remove anything he might encounter that you
  would rather not see reduced to small pieces.

- Batten down loose rugs and tuck trailing wires away
  from his runway.

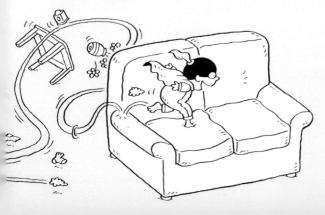

EXHIBITIONIST

Do not be alarmed if your toddler takes his clothes off at any opportunity and streaks stark naked through the midst of polite company – such behaviour is typical at this age and isn't an early indicator of deviant tendencies. Your child's propensity for removing his clothes is not because he wants to be outrageous but simply because he *can*, and running around as nature intended feels quite liberating.

• Toddlers are notoriously fussy about clothing being too hot, too itchy or too scratchy, so try to dress him in comfortable attire.

• Let him decide what to wear, from a selection of your choosing.

• If you want him to put his clothes back on straightaway, turn it into a game to see how quickly he can do it.

- Open all the windows – even toddlers are not impervious to the cold.

- Getting dressed is a lot harder than stripping off, so be patient while he tries to do it himself and resist interfering unless he asks for help.

- Invest in a few garments with back fastenings that he can't reach for more formal occasions or pious company.

LITTLE TREASURE

Some toddlers amass a personal hoard of valuables, ranging from shells to sticks and stones and all kinds of bits and pieces they find lying around the house.

- Respect anything that has been stashed in a special place. Although they may not look interesting to you, your toddler covets these possessions.

- If your child has a particularly special toy or security blanket, *on no account* can it be lost or mislaid, as no substitute will do. You will probably have to wash and dry it overnight so that it isn't missed.

- Crafty parents always have a spare, and a rotation system in place, so the precious item always looks and smells the same.

LOSING THINGS

Having battled for months with her shape sorter,
your bright young spark finally works out what to do,
and from then on manipulating small objects into
awkward spaces becomes an obsession. If you keep
losing stuff and put it all down to absent-mindedness,
there may actually be another force at work.

- Hide your keys or fit them with an electronic tag so
  you can find them easily.

- Fill in any large cracks in floorboards if you don't
  want small items and loose change to disappear.

- Toddlers love throwing things, so it's worth taking a
  peek on the top of cupboards for lost items if you
  have exhausted ground-level possibilities.

- Regularly check the back of the sofa and armchairs
  – there is a whole unsavoury breeding ground down
  there that you should investigate.

MINDING
THE Ps & Qs

Your child's first words are music to your ears but just when you're bragging about how advanced he is for his age, some perfectly enunciated expletive falls from his lips to prove your point.

- If he blurts out a swear word in public you can deny all knowledge of how he learned such dreadful language, but nobody will believe you.

- Your toddler hasn't a clue about swearing, so there's no point in telling him off. He soaks up vocabulary like blotting paper and regurgitates it whenever he feels inclined.

- Your best tactic is to completely ignore it – if you make a fuss, he will most certainly use it again to get your attention, and if you laugh, it will be imprinted indelibly in his memory.

- To avoid future embarrassment, keep him out of earshot of anyone doing DIY, fixing computers or assembling flat-pack furniture.

- If all else fails, invest in a large roll of sticky tape.

THE HOME
FRONT

TV ADDICT

While the odd spot of television viewing is fine, you shouldn't regard your TV as 'The Babysitter'. For one thing, it's far too easily manipulated.

- Hide the remote control if you don't want your set to be retuned.

- Ditto, if channel surfing annoys you.

- Child proof the control panel of your TV and DVD player with a special guard that fits underneath the whole lot and denies access.

- Don't allow her to sit too close – being a couch potato is preferable to having her face pressed against the screen and finger marks all over the set.

FOOD FIGHTS

Arguments over the dinner table can start early, but there's a lot you can do to minimize confrontation. Although your toddler realizes at a tender age that refusing food is a good way to get attention, sometimes she's just not hungry – after all, her stomach is only the size of her fist. Given healthy choices, children won't go hungry nor will they be nutritionally deprived. But if your child is especially picky, try the following:

- Give her a small helping so she doesn't feel overwhelmed (and has less to throw around).

- If she won't eat her vegetables, mash them up and disguise them as gravy or pasta sauce.

- Reward her with foods she likes if she agrees to try something new.

- Experiment with different colours and textures – just don't expect miracles.

- Make mealtimes occasions to look forward to and let her sit with the rest of the family when possible.

- If she refuses to eat, avoid making a fuss and simply remove her plate.

GETTING DRESSED

Toddlers have a bizarre fashion sense. From an early age they favour unusual combinations, clashing colours, pay little attention to either propriety or practicality, and change their preferences on a whim – so quite like the fashionistas in that respect. They are generally united in their rejection of anything that feels tight, and because they have sensitive skin, find many fabrics intolerable.

- To tame your toddler's wilder excesses in the fashion stakes, pick a few items for her to choose from.

- Don't worry too much if she looks a little peculiar – she will probably decide to change her clothes at least five times in a day, so could end up looking halfway decent at some point.

- On cold days dress her in thin layers that are easy to peel off when she comes indoors.

- Avoid the frustration of too many buttons and zip fastenings if she can't manage them herself yet.

POTTY TRAINING

We all know parents like to boast about their kids' achievements, and potty training is no exception. Although some will tell you their child has been using the potty practically since birth, the truth is children can only be toilet trained once they are physically and mentally ready, and anything you catch before then is either down to good timing or luck.

- Wait for signs of readiness to avoid stress and mess. Toddlers can't voluntarily use the muscles that control the bladder and rectum until they are at least 18 months, and some take *much* longer. They will usually be able to tell you in advance they 'need to go' between two-and-a-half and three years old.

- Potty training is easiest in warm weather when there are fewer clothes to remove in a hurry.

- Potties come in all shapes and sizes. If you go for cheap and cheerful, they can be dotted around the house (just remember to empty them); if your little prince or princess is fussy about where to rest the royal bottom, opt for a designer 'throne'; boys' potties come with a splash guard; portable potties will fit in your handbag on days out.

- Some children progress straight from nappies to the toilet. Encourage boys to aim for the pan by giving them floating targets, and provide a footstool to stand on and a trainer seat to allay fears of falling in.

BEDTIME BATTLES

Toddlers consider life is too short for sleeping. They are masters of procrastination when it comes to bedtime. Dawdling and fussing about room facilities and service are just some of the tactics they employ before they climb into bed. Once the light goes out and they are tucked up, a whole new drama unfolds.

- Monsters under the bed are a common fear. Some parents go along with it and chase these wild imaginings away. It's better to tell your toddler they do not exist (but check, anyway, just in case the cat has sneaked into the room).

- Allow your child to have a nightlight if she finds the glow reassuring.

- Establish a bedtime routine – bath, story, drink, brush teeth – and try not to deviate from it.

- Staying in the room until your child falls asleep is creating a rod for your own back. To break the habit, try the gradual-retreat technique (see Three in a Bed on page 44).

EARLY BIRD

Who needs an alarm clock with a toddler in the house?
If he insists on rising with the lark, and you are missing
out on essential shut-eye, take a firm stance.

- Install blackout curtains in his room.

- Ensure he has books and *quiet* toys to occupy him.

- Let him know: Mummy/Daddy is sleeping equals do
  not disturb.

- Gradually shift his bedtime forward by 10 to 15
  minutes each night so he adjusts to waking up later.

- If he comes in and disturbs you at some ungodly
  hour, lead him gently but firmly back to his bed with
  the promise that you will have a lovely time with
  him when it's morning.

THREE IN A BED

Toddlers like nothing more than snuggling between you and your partner. This cunning trick is also effective in ruling out the likelihood of sibling rivals coming along any time soon. With a few well-directed kicks they can keep Mum and Dad well apart and spread themselves out nicely with all their toys. If your child keeps sneaking in at night, you do have some means of defence at your disposal. If he won't go to sleep by himself, try the gradual retreat method below.

- Place a chair beside his bed and sit and wait for him to fall asleep.

- Resist any temptation to interact with him while you are in the room.

- Every few nights move the chair a little further away, until you reach the door.

- Once you move outside the door you are on the home run.

- Always wait 10 minutes to make sure he is really fast asleep before leaving.

- If he tries to creep into your bed in the middle of the night, lead him gently but firmly back to his own room and repeat the gradual-retreat technique.

- If your toddler uses ninja stealth to set up camp in your room, you will have to up your game – try hanging a bell on the door handle so he can't come in without your knowledge.

PEST CONTROL

Adults generally find head lice rather repulsive but they can be a useful ally when it comes to toddler taming – small children find this new discovery so enchanting they might remain quiet and still for a few minutes while you conduct a systematic search.

- At the first sign of eggs or insects, check the whole family. Head lice like clean hair, so it's nothing to be ashamed of. Wash bed linen and clothes as lice can survive for 72 hours away from their human host.

- To eliminate, shampoo the hair then douse with conditioner. Inspect with a fine-toothed detector comb, checking for lice at each stroke by wiping on a clean piece of paper towel. Repeat every few days for a couple of weeks until no new lice have hatched.

- Insecticides – malathion or the pyrethroids (phenothrin or permethrin) – do the business but are not much fun to use. Make sure you always read the manufacturer's instructions.

- Some folks swear by herbal concoctions or an adults-only treatment of tea tree oil and vodka left overnight on the scalp ... but really, what a waste!

BATH TIME

Bath time is for washing off the day's grime, right?
Wrong – it's for splashing about and discovering the
laws of physics. With a bath tub full of bubbles,
beakers, boats and rubber ducks this is one of the
highlights of your toddler's day as she merrily plays
with water and finds out what will sink or swim.
Hair washing is the last thing on her mind and, quite
frankly, a major irritation.

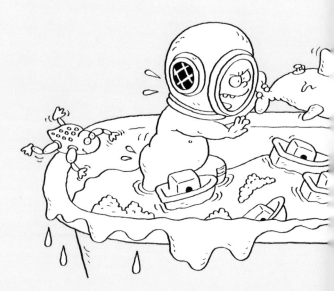

- Don't feel you need to wash her hair every bath time. Once a week is usually enough.

- If she objects to hair washing because it's boring, give her a mirror and let her shape the soapy mop into a silly quiff or horns.

- If she hates water in his eyes or on her face, try a shampoo shield and/or goggles.

- Try washing her hair in the shower or let her lean back over the bathroom sink while you soap and rinse her hair.

- Give her a doll with long hair to wash and style while you attend to hers.

NOSE-BLOWING

One of the less appealing characteristics of toddlers is the 'snot mask'. Once they start nursery or playgroup, little children pass their cold germs around faster than you can say 'Achoo!'. Most toddlers are capable of blowing their nose at about two years old but usually choose not to – after all, in their social circle a perfectly acceptable way of dealing with a runny nose is to wipe a sleeve across the cheeks or stick a finger up a nostril. If your child needs help adapting to more refined society:

- Place a drop of saline solution (available from pharmacists) in each nostril – this might encourage her to sneeze, thereby clearing her nasal passages.

- Not for the faint-hearted – suction her nostrils gently with a rubber syringe and stop short of ingesting.

- Teach her how to blow her nose by imitating you. Make sure she blows gently so that mucus isn't forced into her ear where it can cause infection.

A SPOONFUL
OF SUGAR ...

... helps the medicine go down (so says Mary Poppins) but is not recommended by dentists. These days most remedies are artificially flavoured, sweetened and coloured to make them just about acceptable, although some have a distinctive flavour that is hard to disguise. If your child is feeling poorly, she may not have the energy to put up a fight, especially if she understands that it will make her feel better. But if she violently objects, you'll need to employ a few tactics.

- Try to make her feel relaxed and cosseted – this generally reduces resistance.

- Promise her that she can rinse her mouth out with water afterwards, and spit to her heart's content.

- For toddlers over 12 months, soothe a tickly cough with warm water and a teaspoon of honey and a dash of lemon – this homemade concoction works as well as any over-the-counter remedy.

HAPPY LANDINGS

Having learned to stand on his own two feet, your dynamic young explorer is ready to conquer the world. Stairs are an irresistible temptation, though he tends to be more intrepid climbing up than abseiling down. If he's still in a cot, it won't be long before he hoists himself up and over the bars, then legs it to the nearest vantage point for making mischief. To make sure his breakouts are contained:

- Fix gates at both ends of your staircase until your tiny terror can safely manage both the ascent and descent. Remove them before he learns to hurdle.

- Encourage your tot to come down steep flights safely on his bottom – his nappy provides a great shock absorber, though not ideal when full!

- At the first sign of escape, lower the rail of his cot so he has less distance to jump, or move him into a bed and block all exit routes.

- No self-respecting two-year-old will succumb to being wrapped in cotton wool, so do what you can in terms of damage limitation and brace yourself for the inevitable tumbles and tears.

FRIEND
OR FOE?

BEST FRIENDS, REALLY

Although it may seem like you are constantly at war with your toddler, remind yourself that this is just a phase and focus on the good times when you are the best of friends. One in five two-year-olds has a tantrum once or twice a day, but that still leaves many hours during the day when peace reigns.

- Take temper tantrums as a back-handed compliment – it's only because your child feels secure and confident in your reactions and love for her that she can let off steam in this way.

- Rather than go in with all guns blazing, it's best to ignore tantrums, provided she's not in danger of hurting herself. Left to run its course, a tantrum only lasts 5 to 10 minutes, leaving plenty of time for a cuddle and an armistice before the next bout.

- Watch out for the common tantrum triggers – hunger, tiredness, boredom and frustration – and help your child to develop the verbal skills to express her wants and needs.

TRAINING OPPORTUNITIES

You probably don't have time to go to the gym but who needs to with a toddler around? As his playmate-in-chief you'll be getting more than enough daily exercise just keeping up with him, not to mention the arm raises, squats, bends and other contortions that come with the territory.

- Spend some time every day being physical – the CBOs (Calorie-Burning Opportunities to the uninitiated) are enormous and both you and your child will sleep all the better for it.

- Make sure you have a mix of quiet and energetic games – some cerebral activities will train your toddler's brain and perhaps allow you to put your feet up and catch your breath for a while.

- Start the domestication process at a tender age by allowing your toddler to help with household chores. As far as he's concerned, it's all play and not work so he won't complain.

- Give him a dustpan and brush while you vacuum, or a spoon to stir a mixture while you're busy preparing the family meal. Helping you to unload the washing machine also provides endless opportunities for learning about colours, matching and sorting.

NEW ARRIVAL

Your firstborn may be outwardly accepting of her new brother or sister but, having previously received your undivided attention, she may well harbour resentment towards the young usurper.

- Reassure her that you love her as much as ever and give her plenty of hugs and cuddles.

- Make sure visitors greet her first, before they coo over the baby.

- Even better, ask them to bring her a little gift, too.

- Let her help with the baby but explain that she has to treat her gently.

- Watch out for surreptitious jabs or pinches and over-enthusiastic patting or hugging.

- Try to give her some special time alone with you every day.

- Do not leave her alone in a room with the baby until you are sure she can be trusted.

SIBLINGS

In spite of the gruesome ends that befall siblings in myth and legend, it's rare for either party to sustain serious injury in real life. A degree of rivalry is normal and usually worse when there is only a small age gap (just something to bear in mind, in case you're planning another baby). Problems often arise when a child thinks there is any kind of favouritism going on. Squabbles are wearying and you may well find yourself playing referee on a fairly regular basis.

- Resist the temptation to intervene every time – children quickly realize that starting a war is a good way to get your attention; they need to learn to work out differences on their own.

- Avoid comparing your children when they are listening. Even the very young will pick up on labels and be resentful.

- Treat each of your children as a unique person and respond to their individual needs. Spend time with each of them alone.

- If your children share a room, you may occasionally need to establish border lines with physical barriers to protect an older one's delicate construction area. You may also have to establish 'no-go zones' when it comes to toys.

DIVIDE & RULE

Toddlers understand the power of divide and rule with regard to their parents, so be on your guard to keep up a united front. They have many cunning tricks up their sleeves to get their evil way. For example, climbing into your bed but only kicking Dad so he decamps to the spare room; or turning to your partner with big soulful eyes while you insist there will be no pudding until the first course has all gone.

- Make sure you and your partner are consistent in what is allowed – otherwise your toddler will be confused and easily upset.

- Make it clear that there is no negotiation in this particular situation.

- A chink in either of your armours will spell disaster for the common cause.

- If your partner starts to show any signs of weakening resolve, give him or her the 'daggers drawn' look you reserve for such occasions.

GRANDPARENTS

Toddlers are angelic when their grandparents are left in charge, only to revert to type once they are back with Mum and Dad. You may think your own parents are interfering, not playing according to your rules or most likely spoiling your kids rotten. But grandparents can teach you a lot about toddler taming.

- First, little children are well able to adapt to one set of rules at home and a slightly different way of doing things at their grandparents' house.

- The odd bit of spoiling never did anyone any harm, though it may mean that you can't move for toys, especially noisy ones.

- Little children seem to sense the wisdom and perspective that comes with age, even adjusting their high energy levels to the slower pace of an older generation.

- Grandparents have seen it all before and little children generally respond positively to their more relaxed approach.

- You and your children benefit from time spent apart, so take advantage of babysitting offers.

TAKING TURNS

Patience is not a virtue generally associated with toddlers. When they want something, they want it right now, and having to wait is a totally pointless and frustrating inconvenience. Sharing can also be a trial for all concerned, as the child has to take a big step in understanding that there can ultimately be some positive value in it for him – that is, when other people reciprocate by acting selflessly.

- Sharing and taking turns have to be learned through observation, experience and teaching. It demands a huge amount of trust because a child has no guarantees that if he lends something he will get it back or even that it will still be in one piece.

- Teach your toddler to share and take turns at home, before sending him out into the wider world to work things out with his playgroup pals.

- Sharing with siblings sometimes works better with a timer that pings when the turn is over.

- Avoid potential conflict when playmates come to your house, by putting away your child's most treasured belongings.

COMING TO BLOWS

Toddlers fight dirty – they don't know the rules of engagement so anything goes, though biting, hitting and hair pulling are their preferred tactics. Although it's never acceptable, such unseemly conduct is very common among little children, especially when they can't express their anger and frustration in words. It doesn't mean that they are destined eventually to become delinquent bullies in later life.

- Always make a point of consoling the victim first, before you reprimand the aggressor calmly and firmly (smacking, shouting or biting back will only make violence seem acceptable).

- Explain that biting and hitting hurt and let your child see the victim's reaction. Recognize anger but tell her not to express it physically.

- Treat all acts of violence equally so they don't think hitting is more acceptable than, say, biting.

- Confiscate any weapons and explain why you are taking them away.

- As your child's language skills improve, teach her to ask for things and express her feelings in a civilized way (as opposed to the Neanderthal approach).

TALKBACK TIME

Three- and four-year-olds can talk seemingly without drawing breath, striking up conversations on the bus and revealing the family secrets to whoever is prepared to listen. Often their remarks are brutally honest, while at other times little children tell outright lies, simply because they have not learned to differentiate fantasy from reality.

- Don't talk about things in front of your little blabbermouth if you don't want them repeated at a later date.

- If your child says something embarrassing, you have several choices: you can either deny it, explain it, ignore it or simply look on the funny side.

SHRINKING VIOLET

Some toddlers are typically shy, others only when placed in an unfamiliar situation. Shyness is perfectly normal and tends to be more common in boys than girls between the ages of three and five years, though this trend reverses once they reach school age. Generally speaking, shyness usually becomes less frequent as the child begins to mix with others his age.

- Little children have a big advantage over adults in that they can make social contact without saying a word, so let him take his time in striking up a conversation.

- Retiring youngsters can often be gently coaxed into engaging with others but never try to force them.

- Arrange for him to take part in structured activities, as children can feel shy when they don't know what is expected of them.

- Never belittle a shy child or draw attention to his shyness – simply reassure him that everything will be fine and give him any practical help he needs to join in with others.

TEACHING TACT

Small children have little regard for other people's feelings and make insensitive remarks about anyone who looks different or behaves in an unusual way. So, whenever your youngster's head spins 90 degrees, her jaw drops open and her finger starts pointing, you need to avoid causing major offence by creating a few speedy diversions.

- Manoeuvre yourself into a position that blocks her line of vision.

- If that fails, try playing a guessing game – preferably one that involves her closing her eyes very tightly.

- See who can be the first to spot something (anything) out of the window.

- At the first sign of a 'Mummy, why has that man got a ...?' type of question, bring out an emergency snack to keep her loud mouth occupied.

- Explain to her that her comments might make the person feel bad and that it is rude to point and stare.

PLEASE &
THANK YOU

Teaching children manners is not a priority for all parents but that probably tells you something about their own behaviour. Common courtesy generally gets you further in the popularity stakes than downright rudeness and toddlers are no exception. Left untamed, toddlers tend to follow the law of the jungle, so you need to intervene on a regular basis.

- At mealtimes lead your child by example, such as not talking with your mouth full, not reaching across the table and offering to pass things.

- Remind her to say 'please' and 'thank you' and praise her when she does it.

- Explain to her why people have to stand in line at the bus stop, supermarket checkout, cinema queue, and so on.

- Tell her not to interrupt people who are speaking.

- Let her know that pushing, shoving and whacking other people to get what she wants is not acceptable.

IMAGINARY FRIENDS

Your family seems complete, only for your three-year-old to announce that another person has come to stay – and this new somebody is invisible. The imaginary friend is usually quite co-operative but sometimes has to be kept in his or her place. Girls usually do quite a good job of bossing their fictitious companion around, though boys tend to be more in awe.

- The presence of an imaginary friend doesn't mean your child is lonely, so you don't have to draft in legions of real playmates. Often children use imaginary friends to cope with negative feelings or to keep themselves safe from monsters or anything else they are afraid of. If this is the case, encourage your child to talk to you as well.

- Imaginary friends don't cause any trouble and leave as soon as they are no longer needed. Don't try to force them to go away or criticize them, but don't feel you have to adopt them either.

- Occasionally imaginary friends have been known to take advantage or make excessive demands. Resist all temptation to play along if your child uses the friend to dictate rules or take the blame for her own misdemeanours.

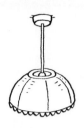

FORAYS ON
THE OUTSIDE

GREAT ESCAPES

Toddlers make Houdini look like an amateur with their tricks, subterfuge and escapology. Part of their success in breaking out from their confines is due to their size, enabling them to pass unnoticed through the smallest of gaps, and hide in the most unlikely places. They are also adept at taking advantage of your back being turned, and quickly learn how to open latches and turn keys.

- Make sure your doors to the outside world are shut and securely fastened.

- Near roads and in crowded places, insist that your child holds your hand or wears reins.

- Let him know how upset you are when he goes AWOL and talk to him about the dangers he can understand.

- If he unfastens his car seat-belt, pull over and don't move off again until he is safely belted up.

SHOES & SHOPPING

Toddlers have yet to discover the joys of retail therapy.
They are on a mission to make the shopping experience
unforgettable for all the wrong reasons and will stop
at nothing short of bribery and foul play to send you
racing red-faced for the checkouts. This may translate
into perverse attempts to lose their shoes, and both
literally and metaphorically throw all their toys out of
the buggy. Supermarkets afford a perfect opportunity
for trolley rage, plunder and pillage, so if shopping
online is out of the question, try to:

- Find a doting volunteer to look after the little monster while you browse in peace.

- Ensure she wears blinkers or practise Oscar-worthy distraction performances whenever a desirable item comes within her sights.

- Avoid rewarding bad behaviour with bribes and biscuits, unless, of course, you really must try on those Jimmy Choo's ...

PARK LIFE

Before you had children the park was somewhere to go jogging, walk off the excesses of Sunday lunch or read the newspapers. Now it's a much more regular haunt and the challenge is to come away with both your nerves and your child intact.

- Parks are rife with invisible trip wires and booby traps to snare your unwitting toddler (or so it seems), so arm yourself with wet wipes, antiseptic spray and plasters in case of tumbles and encounters with dog mess.

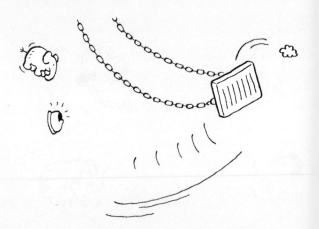

- If mini-hoodlums try to pick fights with your toddler it's prudent to check out the size of the opposition's Dad or Mum before reading the riot act.

- Your child will find a way to flaunt every health and safety regulation and local by-law, so keep a vigilant eye on proceedings.

- Beware of flying swings, jostling for position at the top of slides, rickety climbing equipment and holes in fences that attract toddlers like a magnet.

- Let your child enjoy the freedom of an open space – and don't get too hung up on the perils!

SWIMMING

Although newborn babies are natural swimmers, the breath-holding reflex soon disappears. Water holds a special fascination for toddlers, so you need to be careful around it. Being top heavy, they can easily lose balance and fall in; also, they have no depth perception so don't give a second thought to jumping into the deep end of a swimming pool. Two-thirds of the planet is covered in water, so teach your child to swim!

- Always supervise your child in and near water – little children can drown in only a few inches.

- Avoid incurring disapproving looks from other swimmers by using swim nappies (preferably on your toddler). Outdoors, protect your child's skin from the sun's harmful rays with a UV suit.

- Use floatation devices such as water wings or a life vest but still never leave your child unattended.

- Junior earplugs protect delicate ears and goggles prevent chlorinated water stinging his eyes.

- Don't expect your child to swim properly until he is at least four years old. Before that it is more a question of getting him used to the water and overcoming any fears.

- Join a parent-and-toddler swim group and you'll probably make some friends as well.

DOCTORS & DENTISTS

One uncomfortable experience at the hands of a doctor or dentist can be enough to put your toddler off future visits. Fortunately, your two-year-old won't have any recollection of her babyhood vaccinations so just aim to make any further encounters as trouble-free as possible.

- Try to arrive on time for your appointment – too early and your child will become frustrated at having to wait around, too late and you'll have to wait even longer to be seen.

- Take your toddler for regular dentist's check-ups – it's highly unlikely that she will need treatment at this stage but she will get used to the chair and the surroundings.

- Don't put any negative ideas into your child's head – reassuring words such as 'It's not going to hurt ...' are counterproductive.

- Sit your child on your knee if possible while the doctor examines her and, above all, avoid showing your own anxiety. If you are squeamish about needles or blood, get your partner to accompany her.

HAIR CUTS

For many toddlers the idea of having a hair cut is tantamount to torture. At the first sign of those big, shiny scissors they go berserk. It's hardly a surprising reaction – after all, your toddler knows that when other bits of her body are cut, it hurts, so why should hair be any different? And if she squirms there is actually quite a strong likelihood that the process will indeed end in tears.

- She may be more amenable to having her hair cut if it's done at the same time as yours.

- If the experience of going to a hairdresser is way too frightening, try giving her a trim at home while she watches her favourite DVD. The end result may be more 'funky' than sleek, but at least you will be able to get a comb through it and your child will see where she's going.

- Don't try to force her, as it will only make things worse. If you really can't bear to leave things alone, sneak up while she's fast asleep – a few deft snips may be all that's needed.

STREET WISE

Out and about, toddlers fall into two camps – the foot soldiers and the charioteers. Either way, it can be hard work. If your little one likes walking, resign yourself to taking three times as long to go anywhere. If your child refuses to get out of the buggy, you will pay the price when it comes to bedtime and she's still whirling around like a dervish full of energy.

- Road safety is of paramount importance and it's a good idea to start teaching traffic awareness at a young age.

- Double buggies are heavy and can be a nightmare to manoeuvre through narrow shop doorways. Your toddler may not take kindly to his single chariot suddenly being commandeered by a younger sibling so get your little one into training and build up his leg muscles well before a new baby arrives.

- Some buggies can take a step attachment, allowing tired feet to hitch a ride if the front seat is occupied.

- If your child won't hold your hand or has a tendency to run off, use reins or a wrist lead.

GARDEN SAFETY

If you have a garden, your child will want to be out
there come rain or shine – but there is a slight catch.
Toddlers are very sociable, so turfing them out while
you stay in the warm is not an option. Not only will
they wander back indoors every five minutes leaving a
trail of muddy footprints, they do actually require a
certain degree of supervision outside.

- Clear up cat and dog mess before she finds it for herself, as pet faeces can present serious health risks. Cover sandboxes when not in use so that animals can't defecate in them.

- Cut back brambles and stinging plants.

- Fence off and cover ponds as toddlers cannot be trusted near water and can easily drown in only a few inches.

- Be aware of which garden plants are poisonous, and which ones might irritate the skin – there is a surprising number that are harmful, so prevent your child eating or touching them.

- Feasting on earthworms is not recommended, as the soil they ingest may contain roundworm larvae – try to satisfy your child's growing needs with alternative sources of protein.

- If possible, set aside a small corner where she can make mud pies and grow her own plants.

- Keep her fingernails short and always make sure she washes her hands after playing outside.

GREEN FINGERS

It will be some time before your toddler can mow the lawn, trim the hedge and dig the vegetable patch but it's never too soon to get him started on a little light gardening. Armed with his own set of age-appropriate, miniature tools he will enjoy a sense of responsibility, and getting in touch with nature is calming.

- Set clear rules about what he is allowed to pick, uproot and trample on.

- If you don't have a garden, you can get him started on crops in pots – anything that sprouts and grows quickly is bound to please and this way he might even learn to love his greens – if nothing else, it's educational.

BOOT CAMP

If exposing your tiny tearaway to a spot of military-style training sounds a little extreme, do not shy away. Far from being an ordeal to grin and bear, little children enjoy nothing more than to let off steam by negotiating obstacles, clambering over hurdles and crawling through mud on their bellies.

- All you need for your backyard assault course is a little imagination and ingenuity, plus a ready supply of props such as cardboard boxes, old table cloths or blankets, some garden furniture and a few upturned plant pots.

- As your child progresses through the basic training you can increase the level of exercise to include climbing and balancing acts.

- Finish off by barking out commands in your best sergeant-major voice as your child practises marching orders and drills. Your neighbours may inform the authorities at this point, so perhaps warn them first.

ARE WE THERE YET?

Reaching your destination is one of the most daunting prospects of going on holiday with your little one. Boredom usually sets in within half an hour of being stuck in a seat, so you need to have a shed-load of amusements and snacks up your sleeve to make the journey tolerable.

- If travelling a long way by car, drive at night after your child falls asleep.

- Allow plenty of time to reach your destination and break journeys with frequent stops.

- As well as taking toys to occupy your toddler, play games and sing songs to keep her out of mischief.

- If travelling by train, get a seat with a table so your toddler can get to work with paper and pens. It's amazing how other passengers generously give you a wide berth so you can spread yourselves out.

- Long-haul flights are only for the brave (parents) and the good (toddlers). Start adjusting to time differences before you leave home – try resetting your child's bedtime by 15 minutes a day.

- Avoid annoying other plane passengers by not allowing your toddler to kick the seat in front.

- Keep a spare set of clothes in your hand luggage in case of spills and 'accidents'.

- Relieve ear pain caused by changes in cabin pressure, especially on the descent, with sips of water or earplugs designed for children. Yawning also helps or you can try making silly faces – by this stage of the journey you will probably have no dignity to lose.

HOLIDAYS

People say 'A change is as good as a rest', so, although holidays with a toddler are not the put-your-feet-up-and-relax break you once enjoyed, you can still have plenty of fun, provided you choose a child-friendly destination, plan ahead and know what to expect.

- Avoid places with extremes of temperature and always take care in the sun.

- Find out in advance whether cots, high chairs and car seats are available.

- Make sure you all have the necessary vaccinations well before you go abroad.

- Safety standards and regulations are not the same in every country, so take extra care about supervising your child.

- Don't feel bound to follow exactly the same routines you have at home.

- Consider going on holiday with another family so that you can share the childcare and maybe catch the occasional siesta.

- Don't forget to pack your toddler's favourite toy.

INDEX

Acknowledgements

Executive Editor: Jane McIntosh

Editors: Amy Corbett, Ruth Wiseall

Design: Geoff Fennell

Illustrator: KJA-artists.com

Production Controller: Linda Parry